WATER

Written by

Chris Ellis

Illustrated by

Paul Richardson, Tony Richards, Ross Watton, Zoe Hancox, Andrew Warrington, James Stewart, Gerry Plumb, Mike Gilkes

Designed by

Janice English

Edited by

Linda Moore

Picture research by

Joanne King

CONTENTS

The wonder of water

Water is one of the most fascinating things in the world. Without it, none of us would be here, and the planet Earth would be a very different place. In this book you will find many surprising facts and figures, and the answers to some unexpected questions.

- Why are people like plants? Try the plastic bag test to find out.

- How much water is there in a fish finger?

- Why does a toilet have a U-bend?

- How do you share a drink with a dinosaur?

- What has the word 'horizontal' got to do with water?

- How do you discover the initial of your true love?

- Why is water like a gang of school kids?

- What is so small you get a million million million of them in one drop of water?

- Which creature walks on water?

- How does a lazy artist get water to do the work?

- Who is more likely to drown, a boy or a girl?

- How do you blow a giant bubble?

- How do you use washing-up liquid to make a model boat go?

- When does water turn the world upside down?

- Where do people cook underwater?

The blue planet

The planet Earth could well be called the planet Water instead. If you looked at the Earth from a spaceship hovering over the Pacific Ocean, you would see hardly any land at all. Three-quarters of the surface of the globe is covered in water. Altogether there are over a thousand million million million litres of water in the world.

Oceans and seas   The Pacific Ocean covers more area than all the land on Earth put together. Half the world's water is in the Pacific Ocean, and the other oceans and seas contain most of the rest. The oceans are very deep, with mountains and volcanoes under the surface. Water in the oceans and seas is salty.

Underground water

Fresh water

Water in the air

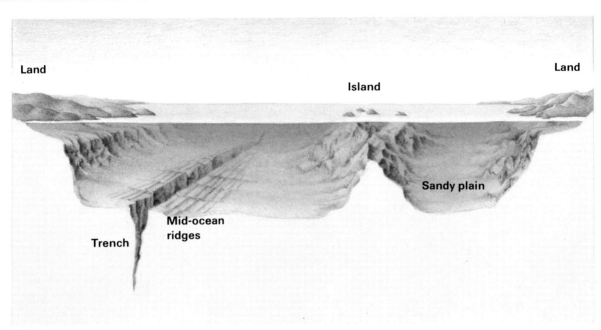

Land

Island

Land

Sandy plain

Mid-ocean
ridges

Trench

Under the ocean

Underground water Millions and
million of litres of water are under the
ground. Rain soaks into the ground and
through tiny cracks in rocks. Sometimes
the water flows as an underground
river.

Streams, lakes and rivers Most of the
water that we need for drinking and
growing plants comes from rivers and
lakes. This is called fresh water, which
means it is not salty like the sea.

Water in the air A very small fraction
of the water is in the air. Some of it is
visible as clouds. Most of it is invisible
water called water vapour. There are
over thirteen thousand million million
litres of water in the air.

Frozen water

Frozen water Some water is frozen as
ice. Most of the ice is at the North and
South Poles. These huge sheets of ice,
sometimes many kilometres thick, are
called polar ice caps. Icebergs break
away from them, and float in the sea.

Ice can also be found on high
mountains. Sometimes the ice flows
down the mountain very slowly.
Glaciers are like slow-motion rivers of
ice, too slow for the eye to see any
movement.

Water and life

All living things need water. For human beings it is the second most important thing after oxygen. We can survive for a long time without food, but without water we would die within a few days. There are many other ways in which we use water, in our homes, farms, factories and many other buildings.

The plastic bag test

Wrap one plastic bag carefully round a plant with lots of leaves. Tie the bag closely round the stem. Leave the plant in a warm place for a couple of hours and see what collects in the bag. Wrap another bag round one of your hands. Tie the bag closely round your wrist. Go for a run or do some other sweaty activity and see what collects in your bag.

Water and people

About two-thirds of our body is made up of water. We need to take in about 2 litres a day, and much more when it is hot or if we are working hard.

Water in – drinking and eating foods with water in

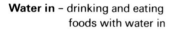

Blood is mostly water. It carries food and oxygen around our body.

Water out – when we go to the toilet
– sweating
– breath is damp, so we lose a very small amount of water when we breathe out

Water and plants

Without water we would have nothing to eat because plants need water to grow. Nearly all the foods we eat have a lot of water in them.

Water in – water in the soil is taken in through the roots

The sap inside plants is like our blood. It flows up the stem and branches and into the leaves.

Water out – through the leaves drying out in the air. Desert plants have thick leaves that hold the water in better.

How much water do we use?

Altogether the average person in Britain uses about 200 litres a day. Think of all the different ways you use water. Making things uses up a lot of water. To make the paper for this book took about half a litre of water for every single page.

How many litres of water are used?

Having a drink	⅓ litre
Washing face	5 litres
Having a deep bath	50 litres
Having a shower	15 litres
Flushing toilet	7 litres
Automatic washing machine	300 litres
Making one woollen jumper	100 litres
Making 1 litre of petrol	70 litres
Making a small car	450 000 litres

Water and food

Try guessing how much water there is in different foods. You have to find:
two foods that are nearly all water
two foods that are more than a half water
two foods that are about a half water
two foods that are less than a half water
two foods that have hardly any water
two foods that have no water in them

The answers are on page 48.

Our water supply

In countries like Britain, there is an expensive and complicated system that brings water to wherever we need it.

The reservoir

Water that falls as rain has to be collected for us to use. One way is to build a dam across a river and let the water fill up as a sort of lake called a reservoir. Sometimes whole villages that were beside the river disappear forever.

The dam

The dam has to be massive to hold back the huge weight of water in the reservoir. Some dams are built of stone, others of earth or concrete. Big dams take years to build. The water is let out of the bottom of the dam through enormous taps called valves. The water flows through huge pipes, sometimes a metre or more in diameter. When the pipes are carried on a bridge it is called an aqueduct.

The treatment works

Here the water flows into enormous tanks. Chemicals are added which make the big bits of dirt in the water stick together. A layer of thick and sludgy water forms in the tank. This is drained off, dried out in huge tumble driers, and the dry sludge is taken away by lorries.

The rest of the water is treated with more chemicals to kill any harmful bugs. It is then filtered through sand and gravel to get out the last tiny bits of dirt.

Water flows down long pipes. Sometimes it is pumped up water towers. It flows down from the top of the water tower to our homes, factories, farms and other buildings for us to use.

Water in the home

The water pipes inside a house make a complicated system. There are cold water pipes and hot water pipes. Houses with central heating have more pipes – hot water pipes connected to radiators.

The cold water supply   Look at the diagram below – can you find each of these in your home?

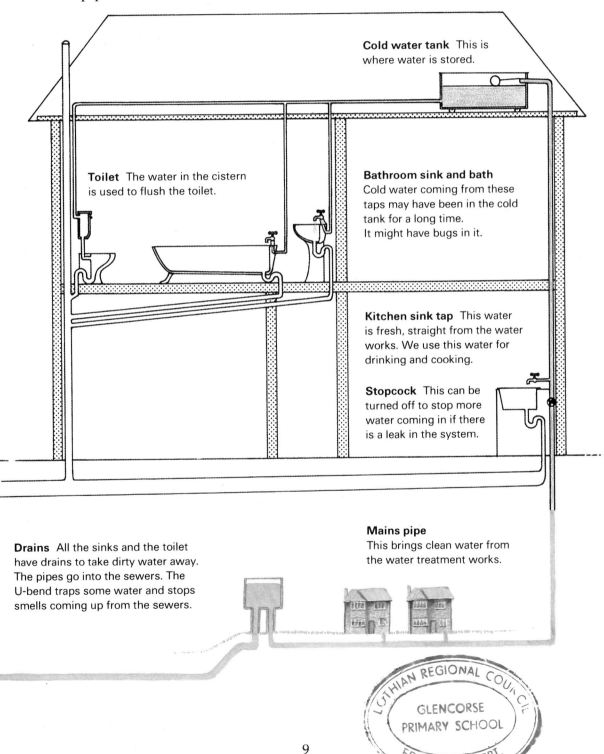

Cold water tank This is where water is stored.

Toilet The water in the cistern is used to flush the toilet.

Bathroom sink and bath
Cold water coming from these taps may have been in the cold tank for a long time.
It might have bugs in it.

Kitchen sink tap This water is fresh, straight from the water works. We use this water for drinking and cooking.

Stopcock This can be turned off to stop more water coming in if there is a leak in the system.

Drains All the sinks and the toilet have drains to take dirty water away. The pipes go into the sewers. The U-bend traps some water and stops smells coming up from the sewers.

Mains pipe
This brings clean water from the water treatment works.

Clean water is precious

In Britain we usually have all the water we need. About half the people in the world suffer from not having enough clean water. Many people die because they have too little water. They cannot grow crops for food, and there is no safe water to drink. Often the nearest water is several kilometres away.

Carrying water   We can turn a tap and get all the water we need. Thousands of millions of people in the world have to go to fetch every drop of water they use. It is nearly always the women who have to do the work. They carry the water in pots or jerrycans which can weigh up to 20 kilograms. The women have to walk many kilometres to and from the nearest source of water.

Laying a pipeline
It is much better if the water can be brought to the places where people live. A simple pipeline can be built with everyone helping.

Digging a well
Often there is good water under the ground but no way of getting at it. A well can be dug down to reach the water. Sometimes the water is pulled up in a bucket. Sometimes a pump is used.

The shaduf has a bucket at one end and a heavy weight at the other to make it balance like a see-saw. The bucket is dipped into the river, and the water lifted up and over onto the fields.

The Persian wheel has a large wheel with many small buckets. The wheel is turned, usually by animals like oxen. The water is scooped up in the buckets.

Lines of stones are used where there is enough rain to grow crops but the water runs away too fast. The lines of stones slow the water down, and it sinks in to make good soil for growing crops.

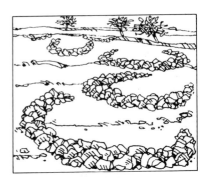

Irrigation

One of the most important uses of water in the world is for growing crops. This is called irrigation. Often the water is many kilometres away and has to be carried by hand in pots. Sometimes the water is taken up from a river and carried along channels to the crops.

Floods

Sometimes the problem is too much of the wrong sort of water. Floods can destroy people's homes, and ruin the crops in the fields. The soil is sometimes washed away, so there will be nowhere to grow good crops after the floods have gone down.

Beliefs and stories

Sacred river   In India, there are many people who are Hindus. They believe that the rivers are holy, especially the River Ganges. People believe their souls will be cleansed, just as their bodies would be cleansed by washing in water.

Water and prayer   Muslims wash themselves in a special way before they pray, which they do five times a day. By washing themselves they are showing that they are washing away the things to do with everyday life so that they can concentrate on their prayers.

Bathing in the River Ganges

Many religions began long ago in countries where water was scarce. Water was seen as a precious thing, which everyone thought was very important. Our bodies need water to live – so water was used in religious ceremonies to show that our souls need to live too.

Baptism   In the Christian religion, the ceremony that shows you have begun your life as a Christian is called baptism, or christening. Babies who are baptised have water sprinkled on them. People who become Christians when they are grown up sometimes are baptised by going right underwater in a river or pool. Baptism washes away the bad things you have done.

Water is important for Jews, too. Before eating on their holy days, they pour water over each hand twice as a way of showing pureness.

New year festivals   In Burma the new year comes in spring. People spend several days eating, drinking, and splashing water around, especially over each other. Nobody minds, because the weather is very hot. To be wet at the new year shows you have many friends who want to wish you success and health by splashing you.

Good luck   Wells have always been important places. Even today people throw money into wells and fountains for good luck, and often wish that the water will bring them good fortune.

True love
To find out who your true love is on St Valentine's day drop egg-white into hot water. The initial letter of your true love will be revealed, according to a traditional English belief. In Greece girls would eat salt before going to bed. If they dreamed of a man bringing them a drink they believed that man would one day be their husband.

Boat race
The Chinese have a festival in honour of one of their leaders from the olden times. The soul of Ch'u Yuan is believed still to live in the water, and they make tasty rice balls for him. Special boats are made, with dragons' heads carved on them. Teams of men race their boats to be the first to cast their rice balls on the water for Ch'u Yuan.

Ice, water and vapour

Sometimes water is frozen solid – ice. Usually water is a liquid, but it can also be an invisible gas called water vapour. Getting colder or hotter changes liquid water into ice or vapour.

Molecules   Ice, water and vapour are all made up of water molecules (pronounced 'molly-kyools'). Molecules are so small you could get a million million million of them in one drop of water.

Molecules in the playground

In **water vapour**, the water molecules are all spread out and flying around in different directions. They are a bit like children rushing about in the playground, hot and energetic and needing lots of space.

In **liquid water**, the molecules are closer together, and flowing round each other, like little gangs in the playground. They take up less space, and they don't move so much.

In **ice**, the molecules are arranged in groups, like children sitting round tables in the cool of the classroom. The way the molecules are grouped together makes ice harder than water.

Clouds from an aeroplane

Evaporation

A puddle, washing on the line, and water in a saucer will all dry up in the end. The water in them will disappear. It has to go somewhere – and it goes into the air. Water molecules float up into the air. This is called evaporation.

Clouds and condensation

If they get cold, the water molecules in vapour join up again into drops of water. High in the sky it is very cold. The water vapour in the cold air turns to water droplets. That is what clouds are. When you open the fridge you sometimes see swirling clouds of water droplets. The warm air around the fridge is made cooler, and the water molecules turn into water drops.

Vapour

Sometimes the water vapour in your breath turns to water. The droplets look like misty steam. It only happens on cold days. If you breathe on a cold mirror or window you can turn the water vapour in your breath into drops of water.

Water

Water flows downwards. The sea is flat because the water can't flow down any more. It is all at the same level. The horizon is a flat line. The word 'horizontal' comes from the word 'horizon'.

Ice

Ice cubes floating in water are like icebergs at sea. Most of the ice is under the water, which can be dangerous for ships.

Down the tube
If you put water in a clear plastic tube you can see that however you twist it, the water will be level in both parts of the tube.

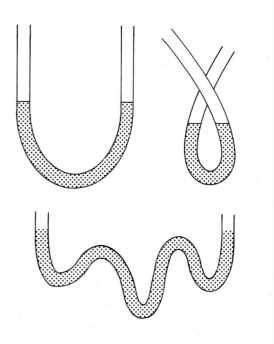

Clinging and spreading

The water molecules hang on to each other very tightly. They also cling to molecules in other things like glass. This leads to some strange things happening and interesting things to do.

Drops

Water clings together – that's how drops are formed. In a spaceship water can cling together in giant drops. On Earth the pull of gravity means drops are smaller.

Surface tension

The surface of water is like a skin – the molecules 'pull together', like a gang of children holding hands. The 'skin' is strong enough for some insects to walk on water. Water also holds on to other things, like the side of a glass. At the edges the water 'hangs on' to the sides. If you fill the glass right to the top and slowly add more water, the water molecules hang together so tightly the water bulges out over the top.

A water drop strikes the surface of a pond.

Ball afloat

Try floating a table-tennis ball in the middle of a half-full glass. What happens? Now fill the glass so that it is bulging over. Now try the table-tennis ball. What happens now?

Breaking the skin

Washing-up liquid or soap will break the skin. Make a tiny boat out of paper. With the tip of a pencil put a drop of washing-up liquid just behind the boat. This stops the water molecules pulling behind the boat, so the water molecules at the front pull the boat forward.

Spreading

The water molecules will pull themselves into tiny spaces. Paper and cloth have tiny 'holes' in them. Water will gradually spread through cloth or paper, even uphill.

Wet towel   A towel touching the water in the bath will get wet as the water molecules 'climb' up into the tiny spaces in the cloth.

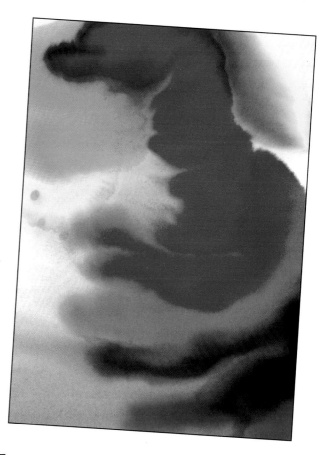

Colour spread

A good way of seeing water spreading is using felt tips. They need to be the type that use water-based inks. You will also need some paper that soaks up water well. Blotting paper or coffee filters are best, but tissues or kitchen towel work quite well. Put blobs of ink on the paper and hold one edge in a saucer of water. As the water spreads it takes the ink with it. You can see that the colours are made up of different inks. For instance, orange spreads out into red and yellow. Try making different patterns and folding the paper to see what different artistic effects you can get.

Light fantastic

Water can produce some very interesting things to look at. If you add a lot of soap or detergent to water it breaks down the surface tension so much that you can blow bubbles.

Giant bubbles   Using a wire ring isn't the only way to blow bubbles. Make four cuts in the end of a plastic straw, and blow through that. Make a giant version using a plastic drinks bottle. Cut the end off, and cut eight slits in it. How big a bubble can you blow? Use the wet rim of a jam jar as a bubble stand.

More bubbles   Try making bubbles using different objects, such as plastic cups, or a plastic funnel. Try to make a bubble city, or a row of bubbles. Examine what shapes bubbles make when they touch each other. Try dipping your hand in the bubble mixture and blowing through the ring made by your finger and thumb.

Rainbow colours
You can often see beautiful rainbow colours on bubbles. This is because as the light passes through the bubble is gets broken into different colours. You can see the same effect in a number of different ways with water.

Rainbows

A rainbow in the sky happens because there is a lot of water in the air breaking up the light of the sun. You can sometimes see the colours spread into red, orange, yellow, green, blue, indigo and violet. One way of remembering the colours is from the initials of the sentence 'rough old yobs generally believe in violence.' You could try inventing your own sentence.

Rainbow on paper

Place a bowl of water so that the sun is shining onto the surface. Hold a piece of white paper so you can see the light 'bouncing' off the water and onto your paper. The light is broken up into different colours.

Magnifier

Use the bubble-blowing ring, or make your own from wire. Dry the wire carefully, and rest a piece of clear plastic bag across it. Carefully put a drop of water on the plastic, enough to make the plastic sink slightly. Now look through the water drop at some paper with writing on. Check how big the writing is when seen through your water magnifier.

Bending light

Look very carefully through a glass of water or a fish tank. Put your hand or a pencil the other side. Things seem bent. That is because light is bent by water.

Try putting the pencil in the water. Try using a bigger container. What difference does it make to the amount of bending you get?

Upside down

Another strange effect water can have is to make things look upside down. Look very carefully at a drip of water hanging from a tap or a leaf outside. If you look closely you can see the world upside down.

Water safety

Water can be dangerous. Hundreds of people drown every year. Most drownings are not at the seaside, but in rivers and pools inland. Boys are three times as likely as girls to drown.

Think about it   The best way to stay out of trouble is to think ahead. Watch out for dangerous places. Be careful where the water might be cold or deep or fast flowing, or where the sides are steep or slippery. Watch out for warning signs or flags. Don't go in or near water alone.

> **DANGER**
> DANGEROUS CURRENTS AND CHANNELS
> AVOID MUD AT LOW WATER
> BATHERS
> BATHE NEAR A
> BEACH PATROL STATION

Survival

If you fall in, stay calm.
Try to stand up, or float on your back. Wave *one* arm above the water and shout for help.

If someone else falls in, stay calm.
Try to find something for the person to grab on to – a stick or a rope or a strap. Lie down so you won't be pulled in yourself.
If you can't reach, throw something that will help the person to float – a football, a plastic bottle. Fetch help.

Danger

On this page there are fourteen examples of dangerous situations. See if you can spot them. The answers are on page 48.

LIFEBELT

NO SWIMMING

Floating and sinking

Some things float and other things sink. Water always pushes back when something is put into it. Try pushing something light like a cork under water. The water will push back, sometimes hard enough for the cork to jump out of the water. Water pushes back at heavy things too, though not enough to stop them sinking.

Upthrust

The pushing back is called **upthrust**. If there is enough upthrust, the object in the water will float. Things which are made of light stuff will float because of the upthrust. Things which are made of heavy stuff won't. Which of these things would float? Which are made of light stuff and which are made of heavy stuff?

Try tying string round a heavy can of food and lowering it into water. The can feels lighter because the water is pushing back at it.

22

Air

Very often something will float if it has a lot of air in it. Try sinking a balloon. The upthrust will push against it.

Get a plastic sandwich box or an empty ice cream container. Fill it with water so that there is no air inside and it will sink. Take it out of the water, empty the water out of it, and put the lid on. How easy is it to sink now? The air inside the box makes it float. Take the lid off the box. Does it still float? Is the air still 'inside' the box?

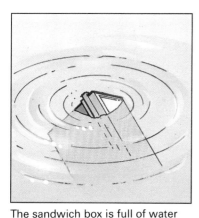

The sandwich box is full of water and sinks.

The sandwich box with its lid on is now full of air.

With the lid off, is the box still full of air?

Stability

Float an egg box on the water. Load six heavy marbles on board one by one. What do you have to do to keep the boat from capsizing and sinking? Pour some water into your sandwich-box boat so that it tilts to one side. Can you ever get it to float upright again?

Blu-Tack boats   Get a good lump of Blu-Tack and drop it into water. It will sink. Now make it into a saucer-shaped boat. The 'boat' has air 'inside' it just like the sandwich box did.

Boats and ships

There are many different types of boats and ships. Two important differences are what the boat is made of, and how it gets the power to move. Boats and ships allowed people to travel further, to discover new lands and buy and sell new goods.

Dugout canoe

Canoes   The simplest type of canoe can be made by hollowing out the wood of a tree trunk. Canoes can also be made of animal skin stretched round a wooden frame, or out of modern materials like fibreglass. The power comes mainly from people's arm muscles, using paddles. You steer by making more paddle strokes on one side than on the other.

Outrigger canoes   The outrigger is a bit like a stabilising wheel on a bike. It meant sails could be attached to the canoes which made them very fast. In tiny canoes like these people sailed all over the Pacific Ocean, hundreds of years before explorers from Europe started travelling around the world.

Viking longships   Early boats with sails usually had oars too, for when the wind wasn't blowing or when it was blowing in the wrong direction. The Vikings had wooden ships called longships, with as many as 25 oars on each side. There was also a big oar at the back for steering.

Viking longship

The Savannah

The Savannah was a wooden ship powered by steam. It was the first steamship to cross the Atlantic Ocean. It had sails as well as its steam engine, which turned huge paddles to drive the ship along.

Sailing ships get their energy from the wind. Some have several masts and many sails. They are steered using a rudder at the back of the ship.

Steamships were invented about 150 years ago. The first ones had sails as well. About the same time ships started to be made of iron, and were pushed through the water by a propeller. Today nearly all ships use propellers.

Queen Elizabeth II The luxury cruise liner *QE2* is made of steel, and has nine huge diesel turbine engines. It has two propellers, each with six blades. It has 500 passengers, and 1000 crew to look after them and run the ship.

Queen Elizabeth II

Submarines

Submarines are boats that work best under the water rather than on it. Submarines stay under the water for weeks or months at a time. They have huge tanks which can be filled with air to help them come to the surface, or filled with water to let them sink.

How submarines work   The main 'tube' of the submarine is made of very strong steel to keep the water out. It is called the pressure hull. Inside it is everything that needs to be kept dry –the engines, the equipment and especially the crew. On either side of the pressure hull are huge tanks called ballast tanks. These can be filled with air or with water.

The Turtle   The first submarine was called the *Turtle*. It was egg-shaped, and had no engines, and was only big enough for one person. The power came from a hand-driven propeller. The idea was to float under wooden enemy ships and bore a hole in them from underneath using a drill.

How submarines dive and surface

1 On the surface, water can't get in through the holes in the bottom of the tanks because the tanks are full of air.

2 To dive, the main vents are opened at the top of the tanks. The air is forced out as water starts pouring in through holes at the bottom of the tanks. The submarine starts to sink.

3 The ballast tanks are full of water and the submarine is submerged.

4 To surface, air is blown into the tanks and the water is forced out. The submarine starts to surface.

5 Back on the surface.

Nuclear powered submarines are bigger than diesel submarines. They have special equipment to make fresh air and fresh water. They can stay underwater for as long as their food lasts.

3 Galley
This is one of the most important places on the boat. All the meals for 75 people are cooked in a space not much bigger than a cupboard. The crew take their meals to their mess to eat.

2 Forward mess
A mess is the name given to a place where sailors live, sleep and eat. This is where about a third of the crew live. Bunks have curtains, and are stacked in threes, one above another.

1 Fore ends
The torpedoes are fired out of the tubes and guided towards their targets by very long wires. Empty torpedo tubes are used to keep food cold and fresh on long voyages under the sea.

12 Hydroplane
This works like a rudder, but it makes the submarine go up and down, not side to side.

11 Batteries
The electricity is stored in hundreds of huge batteries, which are under the floor along most of the submarine.

10 Officers' mess
The officers have more space than the rest of the crew, but even for them it is very crowded.

4 The fin
When the submarine is on the surface, the bridge on the top of the fin gives the best lookout position.

5 Engine room
A diesel submarine has two enormous engines – but they are not connected to the propellers. Instead they are connected to generators to make electricity.

6 The rudder
This is controlled from the control room and changes the direction of the submarine.

7 Electric motors
A submarine has electric motors which drive the propellers. The motors work using the electricity stored in the batteries.

8 Heads
Toilets on submarines are called heads. There are also showers for the sailors to use. They have to be careful not to use too much water.

9 Control room
This is where all the commands are given by the captain. He has two periscopes which help him to see what is happening on the surface. All the main controls for steering the submarine and surfacing and diving are in the control room.

Diesel-electric submarine

Water life

Some water creatures get their oxygen to breathe from the water itself. Others need air, and have to come to the surface to breathe.

Pond skater

The pond skater's long thin legs with their special hairs help it to walk on the surface tension of the water. It can move about on the surface very quickly. It has a beak like a sharp-pointed tube, which it uses to suck the juices out of other creatures on the water surface, dead or alive. It is 1½ centimetres long.

Great pond snail

Snails spend most of their time under the water, though they come to the surface for air. Most snails eat plants, though the great pond snail will also eat other creatures. A snail has one large foot, at the front of which is its mouth. It has a rough tongue like a rasp or file. The more twists there are in its shell the older the snail is. The great pond snail can be up to 4 centimetres long.

Water beetles

There are many different sorts of water beetles. They have shiny hard bodies. The great diving beetle takes an air supply with it when it dives. It holds a bubble of air under its wings. It is about 3 centimetres long. Beetles have three pairs of legs. They use them like paddles to help them to swim quickly.

Stickleback

The three-spined stickleback can often be found in ponds or ditches. It is about 4 centimetres long, and it eats other fish. It spends all its life underwater. Oxygen is dissolved in water, and the fish can breathe the oxygen as the water passes through its gills. Fish have a bony skeleton inside, and tough scales outside. The stickleback also has three spines as protection against other fish.

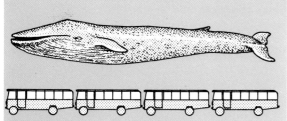

Whales

Whales are not fish but mammals, which means they have to breathe air. The sperm whale can dive 3 metres below the surface of the sea, and can stay down for an hour and a half. The blue whale is the largest creature on Earth. It can be 30 metres long, about the length of 4 buses. It can weigh as much as 20 elephants.

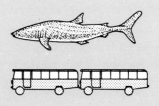

Sharks

Sharks are fish, but unlike most fish they will sink if they stop swimming. The largest fish in the world is the whale shark, which is about twice as long as a bus at about 18 metres. Despite being enormous, this shark feeds on tiny creatures less than a centimetre long. Other sharks have strong jaws with rows of teeth, and eat large fish, giant squid, and even turtles. They find their food by their very good sense of smell.

Giant squid

Giant squid are the favourite food of the sperm whale. They live at a depth of about 600 metres, and can be about 16 metres long. All squid spend all of their time underwater, and can extract oxygen from water as fish do. Their bodies are soft. They have two long arms and eight short arms, which they use to catch fish and feed them into their beak-like mouths. Squid can sometimes move fast by squirting out jets of water to push them along.

Wealth from the sea

Most of the things we need in this country arrive by sea – nineteen times as much as arrives by air. We also sell many things to other countries, which are carried by sea. This trade is one of the many ways in which the sea brings wealth to us.

The docks

The docks are where ships are unloaded and goods transferred to and from trains and lorries.

Swing-bridge
This swings open to let big ships through.

Ferry
Cars and lorries can drive straight on and off the ferry.

Tugs
These are used to help the big ships move in and out of the docks.

Warehouses
Here goods are stored before they are loaded onto ships.

Fishing quay
Here fishing boats unload their fish.

Fish processing plant
The fish are frozen or turned into fish products like fish-fingers and cat food.

Merchant ship
Notice the cranes to unload the cargo.

Oil terminal
The tankers unload their oil into huge pipes.

Container ship
Goods are packed in special containers which make it easier to load the ship. The same containers can travel on the railways or on lorries.

Railway
The trains carry goods and passengers to and from the port.

Lorries loading

Fishing

For thousands of years people who live near the sea have relied on fish as their main source of food. The traditional fishing boats stay out only for a day, and bring their fish back fresh. Plenty of fish are left to breed. Nowadays too many fish are caught by big fishing boats. This is called over-fishing. It means there will be no more fish to catch in the future. Riches from the sea will only last if we look after them.

Fish are caught every day in their millions. Modern fishing boats have huge nets, and freezers to stop the fish rotting. These ships can spend weeks at sea before bringing the catch home to port.

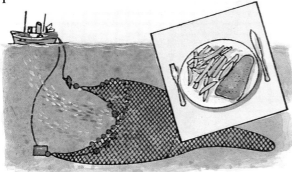

Seaweed can be eaten, and it is used in making toothpaste and ice cream. A sort of seaweed, called giant kelp, can be many metres long. It can grow half a metre in a day.

Pearls are sometimes found in a shellfish called an oyster. People dive down to find the oysters. They hold their breath, and bring the oyster up in a basket. Some pearls can be very valuable.

Oil is often found under the sea. Giant rigs are needed to drill down and pump the oil out. We need oil for petrol, and for making plastics and many other goods.

Water and weather

Much of our weather is to do with water. Air nearly always has water vapour in it. You cannot see the water vapour in the air, but sometimes you can feel it – at an indoor swimming pool, for example.

Clouds   Up in the sky, when air with water vapour gets cold enough, the water forms into tiny droplets. We can see the droplets, but they are so small and light they can float on air. This is what clouds are.

Cirrus

Types of clouds
Sometimes the clouds are so cold the water turns into ice or snow. The highest clouds are made of tiny crystals of ice. These are the wispy-looking clouds called **cirrus clouds**.

Cumulus

Fluffy white clouds can be a sign of good weather. They are called **cumulus clouds**. But watch out for big dark clouds with flat bottoms. They are cumulonimbus clouds. They are likely to hold a lot of water droplets that will fall as rain.

Stratus

Rain or drizzle that goes on for a long time often comes from big clouds that sometimes form a layer across the sky. These are called **stratus clouds**.

Clouds and rain

Sometimes the water droplets in clouds join together to make bigger drops. When the drops get too big to stay up, they fall as rain. Each drop can be up to about 8 millimetres in diameter. They are held together by surface tension. If they get any bigger they break up into smaller drops. When rain falls in tiny drops it is called drizzle. The drops are only half a millimetre in diameter.

Mist   Mist is like a cloud – it is made up of millions of tiny droplets of water. Mist often happens at the end of the day when it is getting colder. Cold air means vapour turns to droplets, and mist forms.

Hail   Hailstones are made of ice. The tiny crystals are blown up and down inside big clouds, getting bigger and bigger, until eventually they fall. The biggest hailstone ever was about 19 centimetres in diameter.

Rainfall

The air over the sea has a lot of water vapour in it because of evaporation. Most rain falls on the sea. It falls on the land when wind blows damp air from the sea over the land. If none of the rain soaked into the ground or flowed away, Britain would be about 60 centimetres deep in water at the end of a whole year. In some parts of South America you would have 500 centimetres by the end of the year. An island in the Pacific once had 187 centimetres of rain in one day!

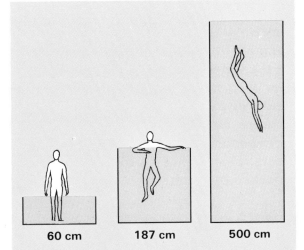

60 cm   187 cm   500 cm

Dew Dew is another thing that happens when the air gets colder. The cold air cannot hold the water, and drops of water form on grass and leaves. When we breathe onto a cold mirror and drops of water are left behind, that is a sort of dew.

Snow Sometimes water freezes round tiny particles of ice in clouds. This forms snowflakes. They always have six sides and every one is different. Try to catch a snowflake on a piece of black cloth and examine it before it melts. Snow is about ten times as light as water.

Water and the landscape

Imagine having a bucket of water thrown at you, over and over again. Imagine bits of gravel and sharp stones in the water, cutting into you. Add a few chemicals to turn the water into acid. Now and then freeze the water into ice. Now imagine the whole thing going on for millions and millions of years. That's what it's like to be a rock attacked by water.

Rivers

Rivers are very good at wearing rock away. The longer the river has been attacking the rock, the wider the valley it makes.

Erosion

Erosion means wearing away. The stones and small rocks in the water rub and crash against the river bank. It gradually wears away. Most erosion happens in storms or after heavy rain, when masses of water come crashing down the valley.

Meanders

Bends in rivers are called meanders. The river bank wears away more at the outside of the bends, where the water is flowing faster and hits the bank harder. The meanders get bigger, and the valley gets wider.

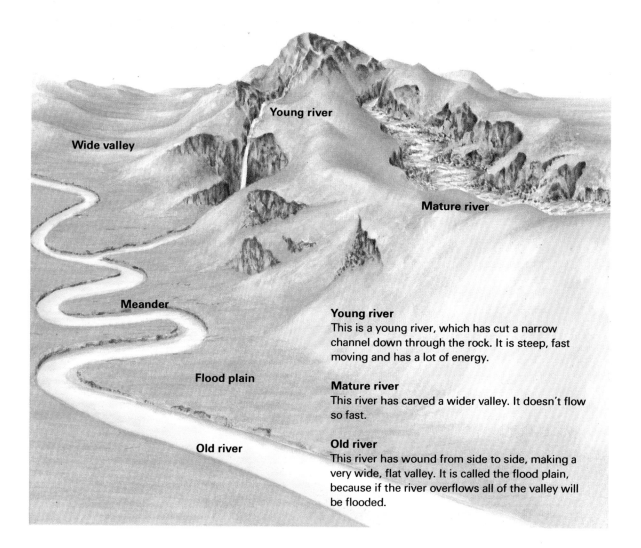

Young river
This is a young river, which has cut a narrow channel down through the rock. It is steep, fast moving and has a lot of energy.

Mature river
This river has carved a wider valley. It doesn't flow so fast.

Old river
This river has wound from side to side, making a very wide, flat valley. It is called the flood plain, because if the river overflows all of the valley will be flooded.

The sea

The sea erodes the land too. Waves crash into cliffs, and wear them away at the bottom. Eventually the land collapses into the sea.

Dunwich The east coast of Britain is being eroded most. Six hundred years ago there was a busy town called Dunwich. Slowly the land was cut from under it by the sea. Houses, shops and churches all fell into the sea.

Defences People have to protect the land from water. Rivers often have their banks strengthened with concrete. Huge walls and breakwaters are built to protect ports from the sea. Sometimes the sea breaks through the defences and floods the land.

The sea flooding Towyn in Wales (1990)

Canals

When canals were first built, travel in Britain was very different from nowadays. Most people would only travel as far as they could walk. Carrying heavy loads of goods over the rough roads was not very easy. You could put 25 times as much into a boat as into a cart, and one horse could still pull it. But rivers weren't always deep enough, and not all places were near a river. The answer was to dig a canal so boats could travel where they needed to.

The canal network Thousands of kilometres of canals were built between 1760 and 1840. The main rivers of England were connected so that boats could travel all over the country. Coal, iron, pottery, bricks, cotton, corn and many other goods as well as passengers could be carried wherever they were needed. In countries like Germany and France canal transport is still very important today.

Building the canals The canals were dug by hand. Thousands of men called navvies were employed. They used picks and shovels and spades to dig, and carried the earth away in barrows. Canals were built in China hundreds of years before they were built in Britain.

Canal boats Most canals in England were narrow, and the boats that used them were called narrowboats. They were 21 metres long and 2 metres wide. Each boat was pulled by a horse, which walked along the towpath beside the canal. At first the boat would be worked by a man, while his family stayed at home. From about 1840 the whole family lived on board, even though this was very crowded.

Decoration Once families lived on them, the boats became more decorated. Roses and castles were very popular, and you still see those designs today.

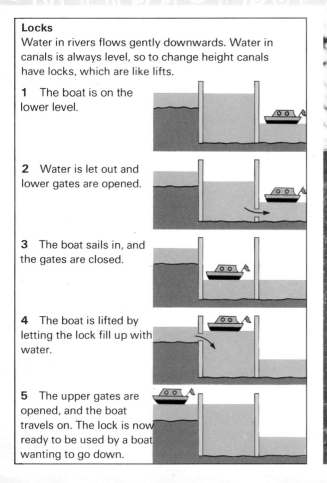

Locks

Water in rivers flows gently downwards. Water in canals is always level, so to change height canals have locks, which are like lifts.

1 The boat is on the lower level.

2 Water is let out and lower gates are opened.

3 The boat sails in, and the gates are closed.

4 The boat is lifted by letting the lock fill up with water.

5 The upper gates are opened, and the boat travels on. The lock is now ready to be used by a boat wanting to go down.

Aqueducts When canals cross valleys or rivers, they are carried on aqueducts. The aqueduct at Pontsticill in Wales has nineteen stone arches. On top is a long trough, just wide enough to take a narrowboat.

Tunnels Sometimes tunnels had to be built. Usually there was no room for the towpath, so the horse could not pull the boat. Instead the boat was 'legged' through. Two people sat on boards on either side of the boat and walked along the inside of the tunnel. They sometimes fell in.

Water power

If you have ever swum in a fast-flowing river you will have felt the energy in the water, pushing you along. Or try holding a ruler by one end in your fingertips, and put the other end under the tap. Slowly turn the tap on, and you will feel the energy in the water falling from the tap. Using that energy to do a useful job is what water power is all about.

Water mills

One of the first jobs water wheels were used for was grinding in water mills. The bread we eat is made from flour, and that flour is made by grinding up corn or wheat. It was a hard job to do by hand. Using the energy of the water, huge grindstones could be turned to do the job much more easily.

Most water mills are next to rivers. Sometimes the water flows under the wheel, sometimes over the wheel, and sometimes in between. Which do you think gives the most energy?

Water wheels

The best way to use the energy in flowing water is to make a water wheel. You can make one yourself using the metal top of a yoghurt pot or a tinfoil pie container.

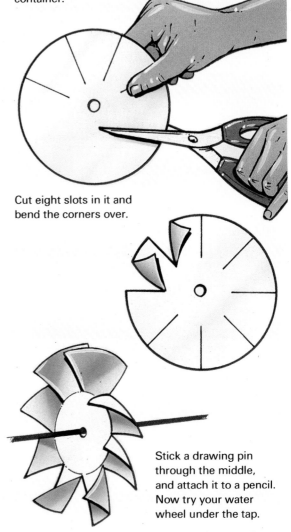

Cut eight slots in it and bend the corners over.

Stick a drawing pin through the middle, and attach it to a pencil. Now try your water wheel under the tap.

Water flowing under the wheel   Water flowing over the wheel

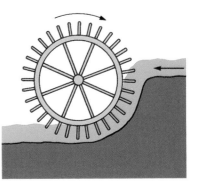

Water flowing in between

Machinery

Instead of turning grindstones, the water could be used to make different sorts of machinery work in factories. The blacksmiths used water to lift their huge hammers.

Tidal mills

This type of mill uses the energy of the tides. When the tide comes in, water is trapped in a large pond behind the mill. As the tide goes out and the sea level drops, the trapped water is let out. As it flows it turns the water wheel. Tidal mills can only be used when the water level is right.

Floating mills

Some mills actually floated in the river. They were like boats which were anchored so they couldn't move. The water flowing under them turned the water wheel. There used to be thousands of these all over Europe.

Problems

Water wheels were very useful, but they had their problems. If there was no rain, rivers slowed down, or even dried up. Weeds and mud could clog the wheels and stop them turning.

Inside a tidal mill

Steam and electricity

If you watch a kettle that has been filled with too much water boiling you will see the lid moving and rattling. There is a great deal of energy in steam. James Watt realised this, and designed a steam engine. There had been some steam engines in use, but they had used too much coal.

How a steam engine works

1 The energy comes from the coal or wood which is burned in the **furnace**.
2 This heats water in the **boiler**, and turns it into steam.
3 The steam pours into the **cylinder**, and pushes the piston.
4 The **piston** pushes one side of the beam up.
5 The other side of the **beam** goes down, and the crank turns the wheel.
6 The **wheel** can be connected to drive machinery or work a pump.

Factories   A steam engine could do the work of several water mills. It also meant factories could be built away from rivers, making steel, cloth, pottery and all sorts of goods. Selling the things that had been made with the help of the steam engine made Britain the richest country in the world.

Locomotives

The first steam engines were all stationary – they didn't move. But if the turning wheels were put on a track instead of being connected to machinery it meant the engine could move. A locomotive has the same basic parts as a stationary steam engine, but arranged differently.

George Stephenson designed the most famous of early steam locomotives in 1829. Locomotives were amazing to people at the time. Some people thought that travelling at 50 kilometres an hour would be too fast for people to breathe.

Railway system   The railway system developed rapidly. The railways were cheaper than the canals, and soon most goods and nearly all the passengers travelled by train. The steam railways meant people could travel all over Britain.

Electricity

Water and steam are also very important in making electricity.
Electricity is made by machines called generators. They are driven by turbines. The energy from water falling inside a dam can be used to turn the turbines very fast.

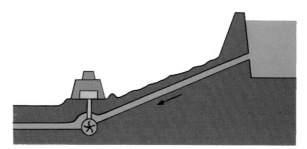

Another type of turbine uses steam to make it turn. The steam comes from water heated by burning coal or oil, or using a nuclear reactor.

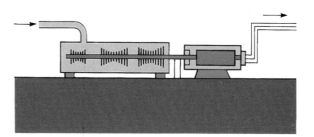

Electricity has taken over from steam as the most important sort of energy. Both of them need water to work.

Water on the map

If you look at a map you can see many examples of the way water has changed the world we live in. Find each of the examples, and say which square it is in. Some things will be in more than one square. Every square has a letter and a number to identify it.

Using a map

When you have found each example, identify the square it is in by reading off the letter across the map and the number up the map. For example, the aqueduct is in square C8.

Find the following:

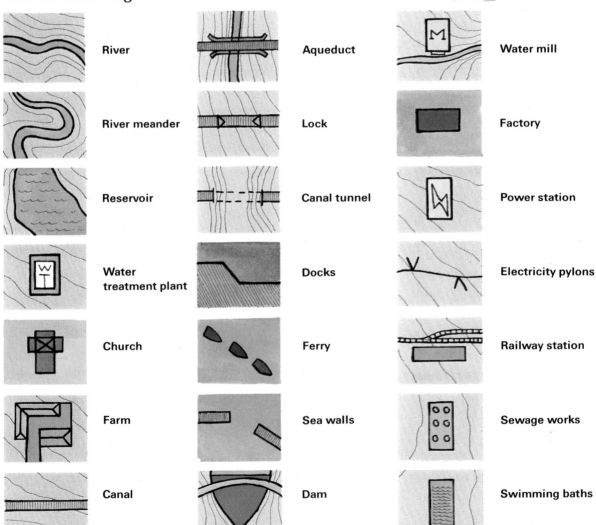

River	Aqueduct	Water mill
River meander	Lock	Factory
Reservoir	Canal tunnel	Power station
Water treatment plant	Docks	Electricity pylons
Church	Ferry	Railway station
Farm	Sea walls	Sewage works
Canal	Dam	Swimming baths

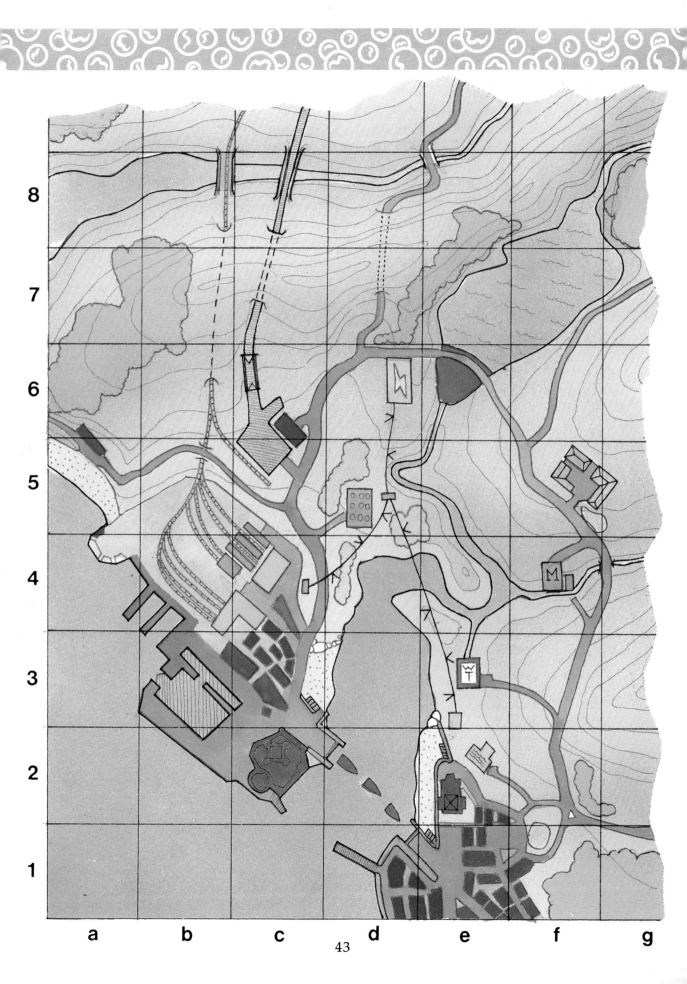

Water and health

Think of the number of children in a class – about thirty. Imagine a thousand classes. That's how many children die *every day* because they don't have clean water – thirty thousand every single day. Water is important for our health in three ways.

1 Clean drinking water
It is not enough just to have water to drink. Bacteria which cause diseases live in water. Drinking water has to be pure.

2 Washing
We can catch diseases if we don't keep ourselves and our clothes clean. Washing with water is the best way to do this.

3 Toilets
When we go to the toilet we get rid of the waste matter in our bodies. It is called excrement. Harmful bacteria can breed in excrement so we need to get rid of it. We use water to flush it down the toilet. The toilets are connected to the sewers, and the dirty water is treated at sewage works or pumped out to sea. The excrement is kept separate from our drinking water.

History
The ancient Romans knew about the importance of water. They used about five times as much water as people do in London today. They built big sewers to carry their excrement and dirty water away.

Romans washing in a Roman bath

The cities Later, people did not realise how important clean water and good toilets were. When factories grew bigger because of steam power, thousands of people lived near the factories in houses without proper water supplies and toilets. They got their water from dirty taps in the street. Their excrement had to be carried away in carts by men called night carriers. Not surprisingly, diseases broke out. Five thousand people died of cholera. Better water supplies and sewers were built.

Dirty water

In most countries in the world water and good toilets are still lacking. There are one thousand million people in the world who do not have the clean water we take for granted. The excrement ends up in the same river that people get their drinking water from. They catch many diseases that way.

Drinking water

Today some people spend a lot of money on drinking mineral water from bottles. They believe it is better for them than water from the tap.

Ever fancied sharing a drink with a dinosaur? Well, in a sense you are. The water we drink is the same water the dinosaurs drank. The *same* water, not just similar. That's because water is never used up. It goes round and round in a circle.

Some of the water used to take a detour through the dinosaurs. Nowadays it might take a detour through a reservoir, a house, your body, and the sewage works.

Money

There is plenty of money in the world to make sure everyone has enough water. In the world today three times as much is spent on cigarettes as on water. Sixteen times as much is spent on weapons of war. The average person in North America uses a thousand times as much water as a person in Asia. Do you think water should be shared more fairly?

The water cycle

1 Water in sea evaporated by heat of sun
2 Water vapour rises, gets colder and forms clouds
3 Most rain falls straight back into sea as rain
4 Some rain falls on land
5 Some rain soaks into ground – comes out in springs or flows underground to sea
6 Streams and rivers bring water back to sea

Trees killed by acid rain

The future

What do you think will happen with water in the future? Will the way water is shared out and used be fairer?

Dumping   We expect the sea to do a lot of cleaning up for us. We dump sewage in it, and expect useful bacteria in the sea to eat the sewage and get rid of it. We dump all sorts of chemicals in it. Will the sea be able to carry on cleaning up for us?

Sea birds   We use a great deal of oil. Most of it is carried in giant tankers and if one of these gets damaged millions of litres of oil can pour into the sea. Sea birds get the oil in their wings, and they cannot fly. They die. Should we make our oil tankers safer? Does it matter if that makes our petrol much more expensive?

The air   Our factories and power stations produce many gases which are carried up to the clouds. They mix with the water vapour and make acids. These acids can kill trees. Should we do something about it, even if it makes things like electricity more expensive?

Sea creatures   Dolphins eat the same fish as we do – so some fishing boats kill them, either deliberately or because they get in the way of the fishing. Do you think dolphins should be killed so we can have cheap tuna fish?

The end?

Water has been giving life to the planet Earth for millions and millions of years. Water looks after us in all sorts of ways. If we don't learn to look after water, life on Earth will soon be very different and much less pleasant for all of us.

Index

Answers: *page 7*
nearly all water: cucumber, melon
more than half water: fish fingers, ice cream
about half: sausages, double cream
less than half: bread, cheddar cheese
hardly any: crisps, chocolate
none: sugar, salad oil

page 21
Small child playing in garden with uncovered pond
Toddler in paddling pool unsupervised
Broken fence alongside dangerous river
Missing lifebelt
Boy fishing alone
Boy running on poolside
Girl jumping into crowded pool

Children boating on rubber tyre
Children ignoring 'no swimming' sign
Girl swimming in canal lock
Children on narrowboat without life-jackets
Girl floating on lilo at seaside
Boy swinging above water
Children swimming when warning flag flying

Published by BBC Educational Publishing, a division of BBC Enterprises Limited, Woodlands, 80 Wood Lane, London W12 0TT

First published 1990 Reprinted 1992
© Chris Ellis/BBC Enterprises Limited 1990

Paperback ISBN: 0 563 34616 7
Hardback ISBN: 0 563 34756 2
Typeset by Ace Filmsetting Ltd, Frome, Somerset
Colour reproduction by RCS Graphics
Cover printed in England by Clays Ltd, St Ives plc
Printed and bound by Cambus Litho Ltd

Acknowledgements
Picture credits © Cover Kim Taylor/Bruce Coleman Ltd; page 2 Zefa; page 4 NASA; page 11 Panos Pictures; page 12 Hutchison Library; pages 14 & 15 Zefa; page 16 Kim Taylor/Bruce Coleman; page 18 Zefa; page 33 bl Manfred Kage/Bruce Coleman Ltd; page 33 c Zefa; page 35 tr Reed Healthcare Communications; pages 35 b & 37 Zefa; page 41 Streichan/Zefa; page 47 Zefa.

© Illustrations BBC Enterprises Limited 1990.
Illustrations © Mike Gilkes 1990, pages 37 (*top*), 38 (*bottom*), 41 (*top*) *and running head*; Zoe Hancox 1990, pages 10, 44, 45; Gerry Plumb 1990, pages 2, 7 (*top left and right*), 14, 44 (*left*), 45 (*top*), 46 (*top*); Tony Richards 1990, pages 7 (*bottom*), 11, 12, 13, 36, 37, 39, 40; Paul Richardson 1990, pages 4, 5, 8, 9, 15, 28, 29, 32, 33, 46 (*bottom*); James Stewart 1990, pages 6, 18, 19, 20, 21, 42, 43; Andrew Warrington 1990, pages 16, 17, 22, 23, 38 (*top*).